Chapter 1: The Concept of Common Sense

Defining Common Sense

Defining common sense requires an understanding of its historical context and evolution. Traditionally, common sense referred to the basic ability to perceive, understand, and judge things that are shared by nearly all people. It embodies practical knowledge and sound judgment that is often taken for granted. In many societies, common sense has been viewed as a vital element of wisdom, guiding individuals in everyday decision-making and social interactions. However, this notion has become increasingly complicated in a world dominated by information overload and polarized viewpoints.

In contemporary discussions, common sense has often been overshadowed by the rise of social media and the media at large. These platforms serve as powerful tools for information dissemination but also contribute to the erosion of shared understanding. The algorithms that govern social media prioritize sensationalism and engagement over factual accuracy, leading to a landscape where misinformation can thrive. As users are bombarded with conflicting narratives, the shared foundation of common sense becomes fragmented, making it difficult for individuals to reach consensus on even basic issues.

Moreover, the education system plays a crucial role in shaping what is considered common sense. Historically, education aimed to cultivate critical thinking and informed citizenship. However, many argue that modern educational practices have shifted focus, prioritizing rote learning and standardized testing over the development of analytical skills. This shift can diminish students' ability to engage with complex ideas and discern credible information, ultimately contributing to the decline of common sense in public discourse. When education fails to encourage independent thought, it fosters an environment where misinformation can easily take root.

The relationship between common sense and media consumption is another critical aspect of this discussion. The way information is presented in the media can either reinforce or undermine common sense. Sensational headlines and emotionally charged narratives tend to capture attention but may not accurately reflect reality. This trend can lead to a distorted perception of issues, where feelings take precedence over facts. As a result, individuals may find themselves making decisions based on skewed representations rather than a grounded understanding of the facts, further eroding the collective sense of common sense.

Ultimately, redefining common sense in the context of today's society requires a concerted effort to reclaim its place in public discourse. This entails fostering a culture of critical thinking, promoting media literacy, and encouraging open dialogue among diverse perspectives. By emphasizing the importance of sound judgment and shared understanding, society can begin to repair the damage done by social media, the media, and the education system. Reestablishing common sense as a vital component of decision-making will be essential for navigating the complexities of modern life and fostering a more informed citizenry.

Historical Context

The historical context of common sense and its decline can be traced back through various societal shifts, particularly during the late 20th and early 21st centuries. The advent of digital technology and the internet revolutionized the way information is disseminated and consumed. Traditional forms of media, which once served as gatekeepers of information, began to lose their influence as social media platforms emerged. This shift not only altered the landscape of communication but also affected the public's ability to engage critically with information. The decline of common sense can be attributed to this disintegration of a shared understanding of facts and truth, leading to a fragmented society.

The role of the media has historically been to inform the public, provide analysis, and foster debate. However, with the rise of sensationalism and clickbait culture in the mainstream media, the priority shifted from quality journalism to attracting attention. This change distorted public perception and contributed to a culture where emotional responses often overshadowed rational discourse. The prioritization of rapid news cycles over thorough reporting diminished the public's trust in traditional media sources, further eroding common sense as individuals began to seek confirmation of their biases rather than well-rounded viewpoints.

Social media platforms amplified these trends, allowing individuals to curate their information consumption based on personal preferences rather than objective reality. Algorithms designed to maximize engagement often promote content that aligns with users' existing beliefs, creating echo chambers that reinforce misinformation. As users are exposed to increasingly polarized viewpoints, the shared understanding necessary for common sense deteriorates. This environment fosters division and animosity, making it challenging for individuals to engage in constructive conversations and reach consensus on important issues.

The education system also plays a critical role in shaping common sense. Historically, education has been a cornerstone of informed citizenship, equipping individuals with the critical thinking skills necessary to navigate complex information landscapes. However, the current education system faces significant challenges, including a curriculum that often prioritizes standardized testing over critical thinking and problem-solving. This focus can stifle creativity and discourage students from questioning information, further contributing to the decline of common sense. A lack of emphasis on media literacy leaves students ill-equipped to discern credible sources from misleading information.

In summary, the historical context surrounding the decline of common sense is multifaceted, involving the interplay between media practices, social media dynamics, and educational approaches. Each of these elements contributes to a society increasingly characterized by misinformation, emotional reasoning, and division. Understanding this context is essential for addressing the challenges we face today, as it provides insight into how we might restore a sense of commonality and rational discourse in an era defined by chaos and confusion.

The Role of Common Sense in Society

The role of common sense in society has historically been fundamental in shaping collective behavior and decision-making. Common sense serves as the unwritten set of guidelines that helps individuals navigate daily life, allowing them to make judgments based on shared experiences and practical reasoning. In a society where complexities abound, common sense has acted as a stabilizing force, promoting understanding and facilitating cooperation among diverse groups. However, this once-reliable compass has been increasingly undermined by various societal shifts, particularly the rise of social media, the influence of the media, and changes within the education system.

Social media has transformed communication patterns, creating a landscape where information is disseminated rapidly and often unchecked. While it has the potential to connect people and share knowledge, social media also fosters environments where misinformation can thrive. This constant barrage of information can overwhelm individuals, leading to confusion and the erosion of common sense. People are more likely to accept sensationalized narratives or viral trends without critical assessment, thereby diminishing their ability to rely on common sense as a guiding principle in evaluating the world around them.

The mainstream media plays a significant role in shaping public perception and discourse. With a focus on sensationalism and entertainment value, media outlets may prioritize eye-catching headlines over factual reporting. This shift can lead to a distorted understanding of events and issues, making it difficult for individuals to apply common sense reasoning. As sensational narratives gain traction, the nuanced perspectives that common sense often encompasses are drowned out, leaving the public vulnerable to manipulation and polarized viewpoints.

The education system has also contributed to the decline of common sense by emphasizing standardized testing and rote memorization over critical thinking and practical application. Students are often taught to regurgitate information rather than engage with it meaningfully. This approach not only stifles intellectual curiosity but also undermines the development of practical reasoning skills that are essential for exercising common sense. As educational priorities shift, the ability to analyze situations, consider multiple viewpoints, and make sound judgments becomes increasingly rare.

In conclusion, the role of common sense in society is under siege from various forces that shape contemporary life. Social media, the media, and the education system all contribute to a climate where common sense is not only challenged but often disregarded. As society grapples with the consequences of this decline, it is crucial to recognize the importance of fostering critical thinking and encouraging open dialogue. Reclaiming common sense as a vital component of societal functioning requires concerted efforts across all sectors, ensuring that individuals are equipped to navigate an increasingly complex world with sound judgment and reason.

Chapter 2: The Rise of Media Influence

The Evolution of News Media

The evolution of news media has undergone significant transformations from its inception to the present day, reflecting broader societal changes and technological advancements. Initially, news was disseminated through oral tradition and print media, where pamphlets and newspapers served as the primary sources of information. In the 17th and 18th centuries, the rise of the printing press revolutionized the way news was shared, allowing for wider distribution and accessibility. This period marked the beginning of journalistic standards, with writers striving to provide factual reporting to inform the public, yet they were still often influenced by political affiliations and biases.

With the advent of radio in the early 20th century, news media entered a new era. Radio brought immediacy to news reporting, allowing for real-time updates that print media could not match. This shift not only changed how news was delivered but also how audiences consumed it. Listeners could now tune in to hear breaking news, creating a more engaged public. However, this era also saw the emergence of sensationalism, as stations aimed to attract larger audiences. The competition for listeners led some broadcasters to prioritize entertainment over factual reporting, laying the groundwork for the challenges that would follow in the digital age.

Television further transformed news media starting in the mid-20th century. The visual element of television added a new dimension to storytelling, making news more relatable and impactful. Anchors became household names, and news networks began to flourish. However, the introduction of 24-hour news channels changed the landscape dramatically. The constant need for content led to a shift in focus from in-depth reporting to quicker, often less thorough coverage. This change contributed to a culture of immediacy, where speed sometimes overshadowed accuracy, exacerbating the challenges of misinformation that would later proliferate with the rise of the internet.

The internet's emergence in the late 20th century marked a paradigm shift in news media. Online platforms democratized the distribution of information, allowing anyone with internet access to become a news source. This shift empowered citizen journalism, but it also blurred the lines between credible news and opinion. Social media platforms emerged as significant players in the news landscape, enabling the rapid spread of information, both accurate and misleading. The algorithms driving these platforms often prioritize sensational content, further complicating the public's ability to discern fact from fiction, and leading to the erosion of common sense in assessing news.

Today, the relationship between news media, social media, and the education system continues to evolve. The challenges posed by misinformation, polarization, and the decline of critical thinking skills highlight the urgent need for media literacy education. As people navigate an increasingly complex information landscape, understanding how to critically evaluate sources and recognize biases becomes essential. The evolution of news media illustrates not only the technological advancements but also the pressing societal issues that have emerged. As common sense appears to wane, it is crucial to foster a more discerning public that can engage with news media thoughtfully and responsibly.

The Impact of Social Media

Social media has fundamentally transformed the way individuals interact, share information, and form opinions. It has created an unprecedented platform for communication, allowing users to connect across vast distances in real time. However, this ease of access to information has also led to the rapid spread of misinformation and the erosion of critical thinking skills. As users become increasingly reliant on social media for news and information, the capacity for common sense reasoning diminishes, leading to a society that often prioritizes sensationalism over factual accuracy.

The design of social media platforms encourages engagement through emotionally charged content, which often leads to a skewed perception of reality. Algorithms prioritize posts that generate strong reactions, further entrenching users in echo chambers where their views are continuously reinforced. This phenomenon not only limits exposure to diverse perspectives but also cultivates an environment ripe for the proliferation of fake news. The consequences of this are profound; the public discourse becomes polarized, and common sense solutions to complex issues are overshadowed by extreme viewpoints and emotional responses.

Moreover, social media's influence extends into the educational sphere, where it has drastically altered the landscape of learning and information consumption. Students today have instant access to a wealth of information, but this abundance can be overwhelming. Instead of fostering critical thinking and analytical skills, many educational institutions have struggled to integrate social media literacy into their curricula. As a result, students often lack the necessary tools to discern credible sources from unreliable ones, further contributing to a culture where common sense reasoning is undervalued.

The impact of social media on mental health cannot be overlooked, as users frequently compare themselves to curated versions of others' lives presented online. This comparison fosters feelings of inadequacy and anxiety, which can cloud judgment and decision-making. The constant barrage of information and the pressure to engage can lead to a sense of disconnection from reality, making it difficult for individuals to utilize common sense in their daily lives. The psychological effects of social media usage have necessitated a reevaluation of how individuals engage with online content and its influence on their well-being.

In conclusion, the impact of social media on society is multifaceted, affecting communication, education, and mental health. As common sense becomes increasingly rare in a world dominated by social media narratives, it is crucial for individuals to develop critical thinking skills and media literacy. By recognizing the dangers of misinformation and emotional manipulation, society can strive to reclaim a sense of common sense reasoning that has been overshadowed by the overwhelming influence of social media, the media, and the education system.

The Shift from Informative to Sensational

The evolution of media from informative reporting to sensationalized content has significantly altered the landscape of public discourse. In the early days of journalism, news outlets primarily focused on delivering factual information, emphasizing accuracy and context. Reporters were tasked with the responsibility of informing the public, providing them with the tools to understand complex issues. However, as competition for audience attention intensified, media organizations began prioritizing sensational stories that would attract clicks and views, often at the expense of depth and rigor in reporting.

This shift is largely attributed to the rise of social media, where the emphasis on immediacy and engagement has transformed how information is disseminated. Platforms like Twitter and Facebook reward brevity and sensationalism, making it easier for outrageous headlines to go viral. As a result, traditional news outlets adapted their strategies to remain relevant in an increasingly digital world. This adaptation often meant sacrificing thorough investigative journalism for eye-catching headlines and emotionally charged content, which can lead to a misinformed public.

In educational settings, the impact of this sensationalism is equally concerning. With the proliferation of online content, students are exposed to a barrage of information that prioritizes sensationalism over academic rigor. The educational system, which should equip students with critical thinking skills, often struggles to counteract the allure of sensationalized news. As students consume media that emphasizes shock value, they may develop a distorted understanding of current events, leading to a society less informed about the complexities of global issues.

Moreover, the impact of sensationalism extends beyond individual understanding. It shapes societal narratives and influences public opinion in significant ways. When media outlets prioritize sensational stories, they can create moral panics or exaggerate threats, leading to a misrepresentation of reality. This phenomenon can skew public perception, prompting misguided policy decisions and fostering division among communities. The sensationalized portrayal of issues can overshadow more pressing concerns, pushing critical discussions to the margins.

Addressing the consequences of this shift requires a concerted effort from multiple stakeholders, including media organizations, educators, and the public. There is a pressing need to prioritize media literacy in education, enabling students to discern between sensationalism and substantive reporting. Additionally, media outlets must recognize their role in shaping public discourse and strive to balance engaging content with accurate, informative reporting. Only through these efforts can society reclaim common sense, encouraging a more informed and discerning public capable of navigating the complexities of modern information landscapes.

Chapter 3: Education and Its Role in Shaping Thought

Traditional Education Systems

Traditional education systems have long been the backbone of educational philosophy and practice across the globe. Established primarily during the industrial revolution, these systems were designed to prepare students for a structured workforce. Classrooms were organized hierarchically, with teachers imparting knowledge to passive students. The curriculum was standardized, focusing heavily on rote memorization and standardized testing. This model aimed to create a uniform educational experience, but it often failed to address individual learning styles and critical thinking skills, which are essential in today's complex world.

The structure of traditional education relies heavily on teacher authority and compliance from students. In this environment, questioning and critical analysis were often discouraged. The emphasis on conformity over creativity stifled intellectual growth and discouraged students from exploring their interests. This lack of encouragement for independent thought contributed to a generation that, while knowledgeable in specific areas, often lacked the ability to think critically or apply their knowledge in real-world situations. The result was a workforce that could perform tasks but struggled to innovate or adapt to new challenges.

In recent years, the rise of social media and instant access to information has further highlighted the shortcomings of traditional education systems. Students today are bombarded with diverse perspectives, real-time news, and a wealth of information at their fingertips. This accessibility has changed how they learn and interact with knowledge. However, traditional education systems have been slow to adapt, often relying on outdated pedagogies that do not resonate with the digital natives of today. Consequently, many students find themselves disengaged, questioning the relevance of what they are learning in a world that values practical skills and adaptability.

Moreover, the influence of media on education cannot be overlooked. The media shapes public perception of education, often promoting sensationalized narratives that contribute to a lack of trust in traditional systems. For instance, high-profile critiques of public schooling and the portrayal of education as failing can undermine the credibility of educators and institutions. This narrative can lead to a disconnect between what is taught in schools and the skills needed in the workforce, further driving a wedge between traditional education and the evolving demands of society.

Ultimately, the traditional education system, while integral to the historical development of educational practices, faces significant challenges in the modern age. As society continues to evolve, the need for an educational model that fosters critical thinking, creativity, and adaptability becomes more pressing. The traditional approach, with its emphasis on rote learning and standardized testing, is increasingly at odds with the demands of a rapidly changing world driven by technology and social media. Addressing these issues is vital for creating an education system that not only informs but also empowers students to think critically and navigate the complexities of life in the 21st century.

The Decline of Critical Thinking Skills

The decline of critical thinking skills in contemporary society can be traced to several interrelated factors, including the pervasive influence of social media, the sensationalism of news media, and deficiencies in the education system. Critical thinking, defined as the ability to analyze information objectively and make reasoned judgments, is essential for informed citizenship and personal decision-making. However, as access to information has become easier, the quality and depth of understanding have often diminished. This decline is evident across various demographics, affecting how individuals process information and engage with the world around them.

Social media platforms have become a primary source of information for many, but they often prioritize speed and engagement over accuracy and depth. Algorithms favor sensational content that elicits strong emotional responses, leading users to consume information that reinforces their existing beliefs rather than challenging them. This creates echo chambers where critical thinking is stifled, as individuals are less likely to encounter diverse perspectives or engage in meaningful discussions. As a result, users may accept information at face value without questioning its validity or considering alternative viewpoints.

The media landscape has also contributed to the erosion of critical thinking skills. Traditional news outlets, facing pressure to attract viewers and maintain advertising revenue, frequently resort to sensationalism and clickbait headlines. This shift has led to a culture of superficial reporting, where complex issues are oversimplified for mass consumption. When news is presented in a way that prioritizes entertainment over informative content, audiences are less likely to engage in critical analysis. This trend is exacerbated by the 24-hour news cycle, which often sacrifices thorough investigation for immediate coverage, further diminishing the public's capacity for critical thought.

Education systems play a crucial role in shaping critical thinking skills, yet many curricula do not prioritize these competencies. Standardized testing often emphasizes rote memorization over analytical skills, leaving students unprepared to evaluate information critically. Furthermore, the reliance on technology in the classroom can lead to a passive learning experience, where students consume information rather than engage with it. When critical thinking is not actively taught and reinforced, students may struggle to apply these skills in real-world contexts, perpetuating the cycle of declining analytical abilities.

As critical thinking skills wane, the implications for society are profound. A populace lacking the ability to think critically is more susceptible to manipulation, misinformation, and divisive rhetoric. This decline hampers democratic processes, as citizens may find it challenging to make informed decisions based on evidence rather than emotion or bias. To counteract this trend, a concerted effort is needed across social media platforms, news outlets, and educational institutions to prioritize critical thinking and equip individuals with the tools necessary for navigating an increasingly complex information landscape.

The Influence of Curriculum and Standards

The curriculum and standards in education play a pivotal role in shaping the knowledge and skills imparted to students. In the contemporary landscape, where social media and various media outlets heavily influence public perception and discourse, the educational framework must adapt to these new realities. Traditional curricula often emphasize rote memorization and standardized testing, which can stifle critical thinking and creativity. As a result, students may graduate with a solid grasp of facts but lack the ability to analyze information critically or engage thoughtfully with the world around them.

Standardized testing has become a cornerstone of educational assessment, but it often prioritizes conformity over individuality. Schools may feel pressured to teach to the test, reducing the space for innovative teaching methods that encourage critical thinking and problem-solving. In a world dominated by rapid information exchange and misinformation, the ability to discern credible sources and think critically is more important than ever. Yet, many curricula do not adequately prepare students for these challenges, leaving them vulnerable to the pervasive influence of misleading information propagated through social media and other channels.

Moreover, the rise of social media has transformed the way students access and process information. Unlike traditional educational resources, social media platforms can blur the lines between credible information and sensationalism. As students increasingly turn to these platforms for news and knowledge, the educational system must adapt by incorporating digital literacy into the curriculum. Teaching students how to navigate the complexities of online information, recognize bias, and differentiate between fact and opinion is essential in a landscape where misinformation can spread rapidly and widely.

Furthermore, the impact of media on students' perceptions of education and reality cannot be overlooked. Constant exposure to curated and often unrealistic portrayals of success, intelligence, and social dynamics can distort students' expectations and self-image. The curriculum must address these influences by promoting a more balanced view of achievement and success that values diverse skills and perspectives. This can empower students to develop a healthy sense of self and a critical understanding of the media they consume.

In conclusion, the influence of curriculum and standards is profound in shaping the future of education and society. As we navigate an era where common sense seems to be increasingly marginalized by the sensationalism of social media and the media at large, it is crucial for educational frameworks to evolve. By prioritizing critical thinking, digital literacy, and a more nuanced understanding of media influence, we can help students not only survive but thrive in an increasingly complex world. This shift can cultivate a generation better equipped to challenge misinformation and contribute positively to society.

Chapter 4: The Interplay Between Media and Education

How Media Shapes Educational Content

Media plays a pivotal role in shaping educational content, influencing not only what information is disseminated but also how it is perceived and understood by various audiences. Traditional media outlets, including television, radio, and print, have historically served as primary sources of information. However, with the advent of digital media and social platforms, the landscape has transformed significantly. Educational content is no longer solely curated by educators and institutions; it is increasingly influenced by trends, popular culture, and the viral nature of social media. This shift raises critical questions about the reliability and accuracy of the information that students and the general public consume.

The rapid dissemination of information through social media has democratized access to educational content. While this can be seen as a positive development, it has also led to the spread of misinformation. Platforms like Twitter, Facebook, and Instagram allow users to share educational materials, but the lack of editorial oversight means that unverified or biased information can easily reach a wide audience. Consequently, students may find themselves grappling with conflicting narratives, making it difficult to discern credible sources from those that are misleading or sensationalized. This phenomenon underscores the importance of media literacy as a fundamental component of education in the digital age.

Moreover, media shapes educational content by framing the narratives around various subjects. The way media portrays issues such as climate change, social justice, or historical events can significantly influence public perception and, by extension, educational curricula. For instance, documentaries, news segments, and online articles can highlight specific aspects of a topic while downplaying others, leading to a skewed understanding among students. As educators incorporate media into their teaching practices, they must remain vigilant about the potential biases that come with these sources and strive to present a balanced view.

The interaction between media and education also manifests in the development of educational technology. The rise of online courses, educational apps, and interactive learning platforms has transformed traditional teaching methods. However, these tools often reflect the values and priorities of their creators rather than the needs of diverse learner populations. As a result, there is a risk that educational content may cater more to market trends than to pedagogical effectiveness. This commercialization of education can further entrench inequalities, as not all students have equal access to the latest technologies or the internet itself.

In conclusion, the interplay between media and educational content is complex and multifaceted. While media has the potential to enhance learning experiences and broaden access to information, it also poses significant challenges related to misinformation, bias, and inequality. As society continues to navigate this evolving landscape, it is essential to prioritize critical thinking and media literacy in educational frameworks. By equipping students with the skills to analyze and evaluate media content, we can foster a generation that is not only informed but also capable of discerning truth from distortion in an age where common sense seems increasingly elusive.

The Effect of Misinformation on Learning

Misinformation has become a pervasive issue in contemporary society, significantly affecting the learning process across various age groups and educational levels. The rapid spread of false or misleading information, particularly through social media platforms, has created an environment where individuals often struggle to discern fact from fiction. This confusion can lead to a distorted understanding of essential concepts and facts, undermining the foundation of critical thinking and informed decision-making that education aims to foster.

In educational settings, the presence of misinformation can derail curricula and misguide students. Teachers may find themselves contending with students who have been exposed to inaccurate information online, complicating efforts to instill a robust understanding of subjects. This challenge is particularly acute in fields such as science, history, and social studies, where factual accuracy is paramount. The prevalence of misinformation in these areas can lead students to form erroneous beliefs that persist even in the face of contradictory evidence, ultimately impairing their ability to engage with the material constructively.

Moreover, the emotional impact of misinformation cannot be overlooked. Students who encounter misleading narratives may feel confusion, anxiety, or distrust toward educational institutions and the information they provide. This emotional turmoil can hinder their engagement and motivation, resulting in diminished learning outcomes. When students are bombarded with conflicting information from various sources, their ability to concentrate on core educational objectives can be severely compromised, leading to fragmented learning experiences.

The role of educators in combating misinformation is crucial. Teachers are tasked not only with delivering content but also with equipping students with the skills necessary to critically evaluate the information they encounter. This requires a shift in pedagogical approaches to emphasize media literacy, critical thinking, and analytical skills. By fostering an environment where questioning and scrutiny are encouraged, educators can help students develop a more discerning mindset, enabling them to navigate the complexities of information in the digital age.

In conclusion, the effect of misinformation on learning extends beyond the classroom, permeating societal discourse and individual understanding. As students grapple with the challenges posed by false information, it becomes imperative for the education system to adapt and prioritize strategies that promote critical engagement with content. A collective effort among educators, parents, and students is essential to restore a sense of common sense in an era increasingly dominated by misinformation, ensuring that learning remains a meaningful and enriching pursuit.

Case Studies of Media Influence in Education

In recent years, the influence of media on education has become increasingly pronounced, reshaping how information is disseminated and absorbed. One notable case study is the impact of social media platforms on student engagement and learning outcomes. Schools across the globe have integrated social media into their curricula, promoting collaboration and communication among students. However, this integration often leads to distractions, as students may find it challenging to balance their academic responsibilities with the allure of social networking. Research indicates that excessive social media use can correlate with lower academic performance, raising concerns about the efficacy of such platforms in educational settings.

Another significant case study revolves around the role of traditional media in shaping public perceptions of education. Documentaries and news reports often highlight the challenges facing educational systems, such as funding disparities and teacher shortages. While these portrayals can raise awareness and prompt policy changes, they can also perpetuate negative stereotypes about educators and institutions. For instance, a sensationalized news segment may focus on a single failing school, neglecting the countless success stories within the same district. This skewed representation can influence public opinion and lead to misguided reforms that fail to address the root causes of educational issues.

The rise of online learning platforms presents a third case study, showcasing the dual-edged sword of media influence. Websites offering courses from prestigious universities make education more accessible than ever, allowing anyone with an internet connection to learn from the best. However, the proliferation of unregulated online courses can lead to a dilution of educational quality. Students may enroll in programs that promise quick fixes or credentials without rigorous academic standards, undermining the value of legitimate degrees. This phenomenon highlights the need for critical media literacy, enabling students to discern credible sources from those that may exploit their desire for education.

A fourth case study examines the influence of influencers and content creators on educational content. Platforms like YouTube and TikTok have given rise to a new breed of educators who share knowledge in engaging formats. While these creators can make learning fun and accessible, their authority is often unverified. The challenge lies in determining which content is trustworthy and which is merely entertainment masquerading as education. As students increasingly turn to these platforms for information, the risk of misinformation grows, raising questions about the responsibility of content creators in shaping educational narratives.

Lastly, the intersection of media and educational policy provides a compelling case study regarding advocacy and reform. Media campaigns aimed at promoting specific educational policies can mobilize public support or opposition. For instance, the portrayal of standardized testing in media narratives can influence policy decisions at local and national levels. When media coverage emphasizes the negative consequences of high-stakes testing, it can galvanize grassroots movements advocating for reform. However, this can also lead to oversimplified debates that fail to consider the complexities of educational assessment, ultimately shaping policies that may not align with the nuanced needs of students and educators.

Chapter 5: The Consequences of a Common Sense Deficit

Social Fragmentation

Social fragmentation refers to the growing divisions within society that result from the increased influence of social media, traditional media, and the education system. These platforms, intended to inform and connect, often foster disconnection and polarization. As individuals immerse themselves in tailored content, they become less exposed to diverse perspectives, leading to echo chambers where only like-minded opinions are reinforced. This phenomenon undermines the foundation of common sense, which relies on a shared understanding and dialogue among community members.

The role of social media in driving social fragmentation is particularly significant. Algorithms curate content based on user preferences, creating a personalized experience that often excludes differing viewpoints. This selective exposure can breed animosity and mistrust towards those who hold opposing beliefs. Users may find themselves interacting primarily with others who validate their views, reinforcing their biases and diminishing their capacity for empathy. As social media continues to dominate communication, it becomes increasingly challenging to cultivate a sense of common ground, which is essential for a cohesive society.

The traditional media landscape also contributes to social fragmentation. News outlets often cater to specific ideological audiences, presenting information in a way that aligns with their audience's beliefs. This practice not only distorts the news but also encourages viewers to consume information that aligns with their preconceived notions. Consequently, the public's ability to engage with factual reporting diminishes, further entrenching divisions between different societal groups. The role of media in shaping public perception cannot be underestimated, as it often dictates the narratives that gain traction within society.

The education system, while designed to promote critical thinking and civic engagement, can inadvertently contribute to fragmentation as well. Curricula that lack a balanced approach to controversial topics can lead to a generation of students who are ill-equipped to understand or appreciate diverse viewpoints. When educational institutions emphasize certain narratives over others, they risk alienating students from differing backgrounds and beliefs. This lack of exposure can hinder the development of essential skills necessary for constructive discourse, leaving young individuals unprepared to navigate an increasingly polarized world.

In conclusion, social fragmentation poses a significant challenge to the concept of common sense, which thrives on shared experiences and mutual understanding. The interplay between social media, traditional media, and the education system has created an environment where divisions are magnified, and critical thinking is often sidelined. To combat this fragmentation, it is essential for individuals to actively seek diverse viewpoints and engage in open dialogue. Only by fostering a culture of understanding and respect can society begin to heal the rifts that threaten its cohesion and the very essence of common sense.

Polarization of Opinions

Polarization of opinions has become a defining characteristic of contemporary society, particularly influenced by social media, traditional media, and the education system. In recent years, these platforms have acted as catalysts for division, amplifying voices and perspectives that contribute to an increasingly fragmented public discourse. This polarization is not merely a byproduct of disagreement; it is a systematic shift in how individuals engage with information, often leading to echo chambers where dissenting views are marginalized or outright dismissed.

Social media platforms are designed to maximize engagement, often prioritizing sensational content over nuanced discussions. Algorithms curate feeds based on user interactions, reinforcing existing beliefs and preferences. As a result, individuals are frequently exposed to information that aligns with their views while opposing perspectives become less visible. This dynamic fosters an environment where people are not just resistant to changing their opinions but may also grow hostile toward those who hold different beliefs, further entrenching societal divides.

The role of traditional media in this polarization cannot be overlooked. News outlets often cater to specific ideological demographics, creating a landscape where biased reporting and selective storytelling shape public perception. This practice leads to a fragmented media ecosystem where consumers gravitate toward sources that validate their opinions, resulting in a lack of comprehensive understanding of complex issues. The consequence is a populace that is less informed and more polarized, as critical thinking and open dialogue become casualties of a sensationalist news cycle.

The education system also plays a crucial role in shaping opinions, often unintentionally contributing to this polarization. Curricula that lack diversity in perspectives can lead to a narrow understanding of critical issues. When students are not encouraged to engage with opposing viewpoints or to critically analyze the information presented to them, they may emerge from educational institutions with a skewed perception of reality. This lack of exposure limits their ability to navigate a complex world, reinforcing existing biases and perpetuating division.

Addressing the polarization of opinions requires a concerted effort across all sectors of society. Encouraging open dialogue, fostering critical thinking skills, and promoting media literacy are essential steps toward bridging divides. Individuals must be willing to step outside their comfort zones and engage with differing perspectives, while media organizations and educational institutions must prioritize balanced reporting and inclusive curricula. Only through these efforts can society begin to heal the fractures caused by the polarization of opinions and strive toward a more informed and cohesive public discourse.

The Erosion of Trust in Institutions

The erosion of trust in institutions has become a defining feature of contemporary society, particularly influenced by the rise of social media, the evolving role of traditional media, and the current state of the education system. Each of these elements has contributed to a pervasive skepticism that affects how individuals perceive authority, governance, and established norms. This decline in trust has significant implications, including increased polarization and a general sense of disillusionment among the populace.

Social media platforms have revolutionized communication, allowing for rapid dissemination of information. However, this immediacy often comes at the cost of accuracy and credibility. Misinformation spreads quickly, and the algorithms that govern these platforms tend to amplify sensational content rather than factual reporting. As users are bombarded with conflicting narratives, trust in institutions like the government, the media, and even scientific bodies diminishes. The very platforms that once promised to connect and inform have instead fostered an environment where doubt and skepticism thrive.

Traditional media, once viewed as a cornerstone of democracy and a reliable source of information, is also facing a crisis of confidence. The rise of partisan news outlets has led to a fragmented media landscape, where individuals consume information that aligns with their pre-existing beliefs. This echo chamber effect not only reinforces biases but also cultivates an adversarial relationship with institutions that are supposed to provide unbiased news. As a result, the public increasingly questions the motives of these institutions, viewing them as extensions of political agendas rather than impartial sources of information.

The education system, tasked with instilling critical thinking and civic responsibility, is also grappling with its role in this erosion of trust. With curricula often influenced by political ideologies, students may receive a skewed perspective on important issues, leading to confusion and mistrust. Furthermore, the emphasis on standardized testing over critical engagement can stifle genuine inquiry, leaving students ill-equipped to navigate the complexities of modern society. As young people emerge from these educational systems, their skepticism towards institutions is often already ingrained.

Restoring trust in institutions requires a concerted effort from all sectors of society. It necessitates a reevaluation of how information is disseminated and consumed, alongside a commitment to fostering media literacy among the public. Educational institutions must prioritize teaching critical thinking skills that empower students to question and analyze information rather than accept it at face value. Only through these proactive measures can society begin to bridge the chasm of distrust and cultivate a more informed and engaged citizenry.

Chapter 6: The Role of Technology in Diminishing Common Sense

Information Overload

Information overload refers to the state of being overwhelmed by the sheer volume of information available, leading to difficulty in processing and making sense of it. In today's digital age, we are inundated with data from various sources, including social media, news outlets, blogs, and academic publications. This constant barrage of information can create confusion and uncertainty, making it challenging for individuals to discern fact from fiction. The phenomenon has profound implications for how we engage with the world and make informed decisions, especially when it comes to critical societal issues.

The rise of social media platforms has significantly contributed to the problem of information overload. Users are bombarded with a continuous stream of posts, tweets, and updates from friends, family, and influencers. This environment encourages rapid consumption of information, often without sufficient time for reflection or critical analysis. The algorithms driving these platforms prioritize engagement over accuracy, resulting in the propagation of sensationalized content and misinformation. As a consequence, individuals may find it difficult to focus on reliable sources, leading to a distorted perception of reality.

Traditional media has also played a role in exacerbating information overload. The 24-hour news cycle demands constant updates, often prioritizing speed over thoroughness. News outlets compete for viewers and clicks, which encourages sensationalism and superficial reporting. This relentless pursuit of ratings can drown out thoughtful analysis and in-depth journalism. As consumers of news, we may end up with fragmented narratives that fail to provide a coherent understanding of complex issues, fostering apathy and disengagement.

The education system is not immune to the effects of information overload. Students are expected to navigate a vast sea of information, often without adequate guidance on how to evaluate sources or synthesize content. The emphasis on standardized testing can further narrow the focus of education, leaving little room for critical thinking or media literacy. As a result, students may graduate without the skills necessary to effectively process the information that bombards them daily, perpetuating a cycle of confusion and misinformation in society.

Addressing the issue of information overload requires a multifaceted approach. Individuals must cultivate critical thinking skills and develop strategies to filter and evaluate the information they encounter. Educational institutions need to prioritize media literacy and equip students with the tools to navigate the digital landscape responsibly. Moreover, media organizations should strive for transparency and accuracy in reporting, fostering a culture that values informed discourse over sensationalism. Only through collective effort can we hope to reclaim common sense in an era where it has been overshadowed by an overwhelming tide of information.

The Algorithmic Influence on Perception

The rise of algorithms in digital platforms has fundamentally altered the way individuals perceive information and form opinions. Algorithms, designed to curate content based on user preferences and behaviors, create a filtered reality that can distort perceptions of truth and relevance. As users engage with social media and online news, they are often unaware of the behind-the-scenes processes that shape the content they encounter. This lack of awareness contributes to a skewed understanding of the world, where echo chambers reinforce existing beliefs and diminish exposure to diverse viewpoints.

Social media platforms deploy sophisticated algorithms that prioritize engagement over accuracy. The more sensational or emotionally charged a piece of content is, the more likely it is to be amplified by these systems. Consequently, users are frequently presented with information that aligns with their pre-existing biases, leading to a confirmation bias that limits critical thinking. This phenomenon fosters a culture where misinformation thrives, as sensationalized stories gain traction while nuanced discussions are buried under the weight of algorithmic preference.

Moreover, the media landscape has adapted to this algorithm-driven environment, often prioritizing clickbait and sensational headlines to capture attention. Traditional journalism, which aims to inform the public with balanced reporting, has had to compete with the rapid-fire nature of social media. As a result, many news outlets have shifted their focus toward producing content that is more likely to go viral, rather than prioritizing accuracy and depth. This shift not only compromises journalistic integrity but also influences public perception, as audiences are conditioned to value entertainment over enlightenment.

The education system, too, is not immune to the algorithmic influence. As students increasingly rely on online resources for learning, they encounter algorithmically curated content that may prioritize popularity over educational value. With the vast amount of information available at their fingertips, young learners often struggle to discern credible sources from misleading ones. This challenge is compounded by the fact that algorithms do not account for the educational needs of individual students, leading to a one-size-fits-all approach that can hinder critical thinking and informed decision-making.

In conclusion, the algorithmic influence on perception poses significant challenges for society. As algorithms continue to shape the information landscape, the erosion of common sense becomes more pronounced. By fostering environments where misinformation flourishes and critical engagement diminishes, social media, the media, and the education system collectively contribute to a reality where common sense is increasingly rare. Addressing these issues requires a concerted effort to promote media literacy, encourage diverse perspectives, and hold platforms accountable for the content they disseminate.

The Impact of Screens on Learning and Communication

The prevalence of screens in daily life has transformed the landscape of learning and communication, profoundly affecting both educational outcomes and interpersonal interactions. As educational institutions increasingly integrate technology into their curriculums, students are exposed to a wealth of information at their fingertips. While this access can promote engagement and facilitate diverse learning styles, it also presents challenges. The reliance on digital devices can lead to a superficial understanding of complex subjects, as learners may prioritize quick answers over deeper comprehension. This shift raises concerns about the quality of education and the potential decline of critical thinking skills among students.

In addition to altering the educational experience, screens have significantly changed how individuals communicate. Traditional face-to-face interactions have given way to digital conversations, which can lack the nuances of in-person dialogue. Non-verbal cues, such as body language and tone, are often diminished or entirely absent in text-based communication, leading to misunderstandings and misinterpretations. Furthermore, the immediacy of digital communication can foster a culture of impulsivity, where individuals may prioritize speed over thoughtfulness, contributing to a decline in meaningful dialogue and the ability to engage in constructive debate.

Moreover, the omnipresence of screens can impact social relationships, particularly among younger generations. As social media platforms dominate communication channels, individuals may find themselves substituting virtual connections for real-life interactions. This phenomenon can lead to feelings of isolation, despite being constantly "connected." The pressure to present an idealized version of oneself online can also contribute to anxiety and self-esteem issues, as individuals compare their lives to curated portrayals of others. Such dynamics can hinder the development of genuine relationships and social skills necessary for effective communication in both personal and professional contexts.

The impact of screens extends beyond individual experiences, influencing broader societal norms and expectations. The constant barrage of information and the speed at which it is disseminated have created an environment where attention spans are shrinking. The ability to process information critically is compromised when individuals are bombarded with fragmented messages. This environment fosters a culture of distraction, making it difficult for students to focus on their studies and for adults to engage in deep, reflective thinking. As society grapples with these changes, there is a pressing need to cultivate digital literacy skills that empower individuals to navigate the complexities of the information age effectively.

In light of these challenges, it is crucial for educators, parents, and policymakers to reevaluate the role of screens in learning and communication. Finding a balance between technology use and traditional educational practices can enhance learning outcomes while preserving the essential skills needed for effective communication. By fostering environments that encourage critical thinking, empathy, and meaningful interactions, it is possible to mitigate the adverse effects of screens on society. Emphasizing the importance of common sense in navigating the digital landscape can help ensure that future generations are equipped to thrive in an increasingly complex world influenced by social media, the media, and the evolving education system.

Chapter 7: Reclaiming Common Sense

Strategies for Critical Thinking

Critical thinking is an essential skill that enables individuals to analyze information, evaluate arguments, and make informed decisions. In a world inundated with social media noise, sensational news, and often flawed educational paradigms, cultivating critical thinking skills is more important than ever. Strategies that promote critical thinking can empower individuals to sift through the vast amounts of information they encounter daily and discern what is credible and relevant.

One effective strategy is to practice questioning assumptions. Many people accept information at face value without scrutinizing its origin or context. By routinely asking questions such as "What evidence supports this claim?" or "Could there be an alternative perspective?" individuals can challenge their own biases and preconceptions. This process not only enhances analytical skills but also encourages a more nuanced understanding of complex issues. Engaging in discussions that promote inquiry can further reinforce this habit, allowing individuals to explore diverse viewpoints.

Another vital strategy for fostering critical thinking is to develop strong research skills. In an age where misinformation can spread rapidly, knowing how to identify reliable sources is crucial. Individuals should learn to distinguish between credible evidence and mere opinion. This involves understanding the difference between primary and secondary sources, evaluating the qualifications of authors, and recognizing potential biases in reporting. By honing their research abilities, individuals can better navigate the information landscape and avoid falling prey to misleading narratives.

Additionally, engaging in reflective thinking can significantly enhance critical thinking capabilities. Taking time to reflect on one's own thought processes allows individuals to recognize their cognitive biases and emotional responses to information. Journaling or discussing thoughts with others can provide insight into how one's background influences their understanding of issues. This reflective practice not only promotes self-awareness but also encourages a more objective approach to evaluating information, leading to clearer, more rational decision-making.

Finally, collaboration with others can be a powerful tool for developing critical thinking skills. Participating in group discussions or collaborative projects encourages individuals to articulate their thoughts and consider feedback from peers. This interaction fosters a dynamic exchange of ideas, where individuals are challenged to defend their viewpoints and consider alternative perspectives. Such collaborative environments can stimulate deeper analysis and encourage a culture of critical inquiry, ultimately cultivating a more discerning public capable of navigating the complexities of modern information.

The Importance of Media Literacy

The landscape of information consumption has dramatically shifted in the digital age, making media literacy an essential skill for individuals of all ages. In an era dominated by social media, where news and information can be disseminated and consumed at lightning speed, the ability to critically evaluate sources and understand the nuances of media messages is paramount. Media literacy empowers individuals to navigate the complexities of information, discern fact from fiction, and develop informed opinions, which is increasingly vital in a world rife with misinformation and propaganda.

One of the primary reasons media literacy is crucial today is the overwhelming presence of social media platforms that serve as major news sources for many. These platforms often prioritize engagement over accuracy, leading to the rapid spread of sensationalized content and false narratives. Without the skills to critically assess these messages, individuals may unwittingly contribute to the dissemination of misleading information. Developing media literacy skills can help users identify credible sources, recognize bias, and understand the context behind the information they encounter, fostering a more informed and responsible citizenry.

Furthermore, the education system plays a significant role in shaping media literacy among younger generations. Despite the pervasive influence of digital media, traditional educational curricula often neglect to address the need for critical thinking regarding media consumption. By integrating media literacy into educational programs, schools can equip students with the tools necessary to analyze media critically and understand its impact on society. This foundation not only prepares students to engage thoughtfully with media but also encourages them to become active participants in democratic discourse, challenging the status quo and advocating for truth and accountability.

Moreover, the implications of media literacy extend beyond individual understanding; they influence the broader societal landscape. A media-literate population is better equipped to engage in constructive dialogue, question narratives propagated by those in power, and demand transparency from media organizations. This collective awareness can lead to a more informed electorate that is less susceptible to manipulation and more resilient against divisive rhetoric. In a time when polarization and mistrust are rampant, promoting media literacy is a pathway toward fostering a more cohesive society.

In conclusion, the importance of media literacy cannot be overstated in today's information-saturated environment. It serves as a critical tool for individuals to navigate the complexities of the media landscape, empowering them to make informed choices and contribute meaningfully to public discourse. By prioritizing media literacy in both personal and educational contexts, we can cultivate a society that values common sense, critical thinking, and informed citizenship, ultimately working towards a healthier democratic process.

Educational Reforms for the Future

Educational reforms for the future must address the profound impact that social media, traditional media, and the current education system have on critical thinking and the ability to discern credible information. The digital age has transformed the way information is consumed, often leading to the spread of misinformation. This necessitates a re-evaluation of educational priorities, emphasizing the development of critical thinking skills. Schools should focus on teaching students how to assess sources, analyze arguments, and engage in constructive dialogue, preparing them for a world inundated with information.

One key aspect of reform is integrating digital literacy into the curriculum. As students increasingly rely on social media for news and information, they must be equipped with the tools to navigate this landscape. Digital literacy education should cover not only how to identify reliable information but also how to understand algorithms and the influence of social media on public perception. By incorporating these topics into existing subjects, educators can foster an informed generation capable of making sound judgments about the information they encounter.

Furthermore, the role of educators must evolve in response to these changes. Teachers should be trained not only in content delivery but also in facilitating discussions around media literacy and critical thinking. Professional development programs can provide educators with strategies to engage students in analyzing media messages and fostering a classroom environment that encourages questioning and debate. This shift in teaching methodology will empower students to become active participants in their education, rather than passive consumers of information.

Another crucial component of educational reform is promoting interdisciplinary learning. Many of the challenges faced by society today, including those stemming from misinformation, require a multifaceted approach. By breaking down the barriers between subjects like science, social studies, and language arts, students can develop a more holistic understanding of complex issues. This integrated approach encourages students to draw connections between different fields of study, enhancing their ability to think critically and creatively about the world around them.

Lastly, engaging parents and communities in the educational reform process is essential. Schools should create partnerships with families and local organizations to promote a culture of critical inquiry and media literacy beyond the classroom. Community workshops, public discussions, and collaborative projects can help reinforce the skills students learn in school. By working together, educators, parents, and community members can foster an environment that values common sense and critical thinking, ultimately reversing the trend of misinformation and its detrimental effects on society.

Chapter 8: A Call to Action

Engaging Communities

Engaging communities in today's world requires a nuanced understanding of how social media, traditional media, and the education system interact to shape public discourse. The proliferation of social media platforms has altered the way communities connect and communicate. While these platforms offer unprecedented opportunities for interaction, they also present challenges, such as the spread of misinformation and the polarization of opinions. To effectively engage communities, it is essential to recognize these dynamics and develop strategies that foster genuine dialogue and collective action.

One effective approach to community engagement is the emphasis on local initiatives that harness the power of social media. Grassroots movements can thrive when individuals come together online to share their experiences, concerns, and ideas. Initiatives that focus on local needs and values can create a sense of belonging and empower community members. By utilizing social media tools to promote local events, share success stories, and provide updates on community projects, organizers can strengthen ties among residents and encourage active participation.

Moreover, traditional media still plays a crucial role in engaging communities, especially when it comes to informing the public about important issues. Local newspapers, radio stations, and television channels can serve as platforms for discussion, providing context and fostering understanding around complex topics. By partnering with local media outlets, community leaders can amplify their messages and reach broader audiences. This collaboration can help bridge gaps in knowledge and counteract the effects of misinformation that often proliferates on social media.

The education system is also a vital player in community engagement. Schools and educational institutions can serve as hubs for civic engagement, encouraging students to participate in community service and local governance. By integrating community issues into the curriculum, educators can help students develop critical thinking skills and a sense of responsibility toward their communities. This proactive approach not only prepares students for active citizenship but also fosters a culture of engagement that extends beyond the classroom.

Finally, fostering a culture of engagement requires ongoing commitment from all stakeholders, including community members, educators, and media professionals. Training programs, workshops, and community forums can provide individuals with the tools and knowledge necessary to engage effectively. Encouraging open dialogue, respect for diverse perspectives, and a commitment to shared values can create an environment where communities thrive. In a world where common sense often seems elusive, prioritizing engagement can help revitalize public discourse and promote a more informed and connected society.

Encouraging Responsible Media Consumption

Encouraging responsible media consumption is crucial in today's digital landscape, where information is abundant yet often misleading. The rapid rise of social media platforms has transformed the way we access and interact with information. Users are bombarded with a continuous stream of content that varies widely in quality and accuracy. This environment necessitates a proactive approach to media consumption, emphasizing critical thinking and discernment among consumers of all ages.

To foster responsible media consumption, education plays a vital role. Schools should integrate media literacy into their curricula, teaching students how to analyze sources, identify bias, and understand the motivations behind different types of content. By equipping young individuals with these skills, we can help them navigate the complex media landscape more effectively. This education should not be limited to formal institutions; parents and guardians also have a responsibility to engage in discussions about media consumption with their children, modeling critical evaluation of information from an early age.

Another key aspect of responsible media consumption is the importance of diversifying information sources. Relying on a single platform or outlet can create echo chambers that reinforce existing beliefs while excluding alternative perspectives. Encouraging individuals to seek out a range of viewpoints can enhance their understanding of issues and foster empathy. This practice not only broadens one's knowledge but also cultivates a more informed citizenry capable of engaging in constructive discourse about pressing social and political issues.

Moreover, consumers should develop a habit of fact-checking before sharing content. The viral nature of social media often leads to the rapid spread of misinformation, which can have serious consequences. By taking a moment to verify the authenticity of a story or claim, individuals can significantly reduce the risk of perpetuating falsehoods. Fact-checking resources are widely available and should be utilized as a standard practice, encouraging a culture of accountability and responsibility in media sharing.

Finally, promoting mindfulness in media consumption can lead to healthier engagement with information. Encouraging individuals to reflect on their motivations for consuming certain content can help them make more intentional choices. This involves recognizing emotional triggers, such as outrage or fear, that often drive engagement with sensationalized media. By prioritizing quality over quantity and being aware of the effects of media on mental health, individuals can cultivate a more balanced relationship with information, ultimately fostering a society that values truth and critical thinking over sensationalism.

Building a New Educational Paradigm

The concept of a new educational paradigm is essential in addressing the current crises in our education system, largely influenced by social media and traditional media narratives. This paradigm shift requires a comprehensive reevaluation of how education is delivered, focusing on critical thinking, creativity, and emotional intelligence rather than rote memorization and standardized testing. As the digital landscape continues to evolve, educators must adapt their methodologies to foster skills that are relevant in a rapidly changing world. The goal is to cultivate learners who are not only knowledgeable but also capable of navigating complex societal issues with discernment.

One of the cornerstones of this new educational framework is the integration of technology in a way that enhances learning rather than detracts from it. Social media platforms, while often criticized for their negative impact on attention spans and critical thinking, can also serve as powerful tools for engagement and collaboration. By leveraging these platforms to create interactive learning experiences, educators can encourage students to explore diverse perspectives, engage in meaningful dialogue, and develop digital literacy skills essential for the modern workforce. This approach not only makes learning more relevant but also prepares students to critically evaluate the information they encounter online.

Moreover, the role of educators must evolve from mere dispensers of knowledge to facilitators of learning. In this new paradigm, teachers will guide students in inquiry-based learning, where curiosity drives exploration and discovery. This method fosters an environment where students feel empowered to ask questions, challenge assumptions, and pursue their interests. By prioritizing student agency, educators can help learners develop a sense of ownership over their education, which is crucial in cultivating lifelong learners who can think critically about the world around them.

Additionally, addressing the emotional and social aspects of learning is vital in this new educational model. The impact of social media on mental health and self-perception cannot be overlooked. Schools must prioritize social-emotional learning (SEL) to equip students with the tools to manage their emotions, build healthy relationships, and make responsible decisions. Integrating SEL into the curriculum not only supports students' overall well-being but also fosters a more inclusive and empathetic school culture, which is essential in counteracting the divisiveness often seen in online interactions.

Lastly, community involvement and collaboration are essential components of a successful educational paradigm. Engaging parents, local organizations, and industry leaders in the educational process creates a support network that enriches student learning experiences. By fostering partnerships between schools and communities, educators can provide students with real-world applications of their knowledge, helping them understand the relevance of their education. This collaborative approach not only enhances academic outcomes but also bridges the gap between education and the realities of life beyond the classroom, preparing students to navigate the complexities of the modern world.

Chapter 9: Looking Ahead

The Future of Common Sense

The future of common sense is a topic that demands urgent attention as society grapples with the profound changes brought about by social media, traditional media, and educational frameworks. Common sense, once a shared understanding that guided human interaction and decision-making, is increasingly overshadowed by misinformation, sensationalism, and polarized narratives. As these influences become more pervasive, the challenge lies in reviving the principles of common sense amidst an environment that often prioritizes engagement over accuracy.

Social media platforms have transformed the way information is disseminated and consumed. In a landscape where viral content often eclipses factual reporting, users are bombarded with a continuous stream of opinions rather than informed discourse. Algorithms prioritize sensational content, creating echo chambers that reinforce existing beliefs rather than challenge them. As a result, common sense reasoning is often replaced by emotional responses, leading to a diminished capacity for critical thinking and rational dialogue. The future of common sense hinges on our ability to navigate this digital terrain and cultivate a culture that values thoughtful engagement over superficial interactions.

The role of traditional media cannot be overlooked in this discourse. As news outlets compete for viewership and clicks, the line between journalism and entertainment has blurred. The emphasis on sensational headlines and clickbait has contributed to an erosion of trust in media sources, prompting audiences to seek validation for their biases rather than objective truth. This shift has profound implications for common sense, as it fosters an environment where misinformation thrives and critical analysis is sidelined. Addressing this issue requires a concerted effort from media organizations to prioritize integrity and accountability, ensuring that the information disseminated serves the public interest rather than mere profit.

Educational systems also play a crucial role in shaping the future of common sense. A curriculum focused on rote memorization and standardized testing often neglects the development of critical thinking skills necessary for navigating complex societal issues. To revive common sense, educational institutions must prioritize teaching students how to analyze information, evaluate sources, and engage in constructive dialogue. By equipping future generations with the tools to think critically and engage thoughtfully, we can foster a culture where common sense is not only valued but actively practiced.

The future of common sense will ultimately depend on individuals' commitment to seeking truth and engaging with diverse perspectives. It calls for a collective responsibility to challenge the status quo, question assumptions, and prioritize informed dialogue over divisive rhetoric. As society continues to evolve in the face of technological and cultural shifts, the revival of common sense is not merely a nostalgic longing for the past but a necessary pursuit for a more rational and cohesive future. Embracing this challenge will require vigilance, education, and a willingness to engage in the hard work of rebuilding a shared understanding that serves the greater good.

The Role of Individuals in Change

The role of individuals in driving change is pivotal in a society increasingly influenced by social media, mainstream media, and educational institutions. While these entities often shape narratives and public opinion, individuals possess the unique ability to resist, adapt, and create alternative perspectives. The collective actions of individuals can challenge prevailing norms, promote critical thinking, and ultimately influence the broader societal landscape. It is essential to recognize that personal agency can catalyze significant changes, especially in an era where common sense appears to be overshadowed by sensationalism and misinformation.

Individuals can leverage social media platforms to amplify their voices and foster communities around shared values and ideas. This democratization of information allows for diverse viewpoints to emerge, challenging the singular narratives often propagated by traditional media outlets. By engaging in thoughtful discourse, sharing credible information, and promoting educational content, individuals can contribute to a more informed society. The potential for grassroots movements to gain momentum demonstrates how individual actions can lead to widespread change, highlighting the power of personal responsibility in the digital age.

Moreover, individuals play a crucial role in combating the misinformation that pervades social media and other media channels. By prioritizing critical thinking and media literacy, people can discern credible sources from unreliable ones. This vigilance not only protects personal beliefs but also fosters a culture of accountability within communities. When individuals actively question and fact-check the information they encounter, they contribute to a more discerning public, counteracting the careless consumption of content that often leads to the erosion of common sense.

Education, too, is an area where individuals can effect change. While formal education systems may sometimes perpetuate outdated ideas or suppress critical inquiry, individuals have the power to seek alternative forms of learning. Engaging in self-directed education, participating in community discussions, or pursuing lifelong learning can cultivate a more discerning mindset. By challenging the status quo and advocating for curricula that emphasize critical thinking and real-world applications, individuals can help reshape educational priorities and outcomes, ultimately influencing future generations.

In summary, the role of individuals in driving change is multifaceted and essential in an era marked by the decline of common sense. By leveraging social media for constructive dialogue, combating misinformation through critical engagement, and advocating for transformative educational practices, individuals can reclaim agency in a world that often seems dominated by external influences. The collective efforts of individuals can pave the way for a more rational and informed society, reinforcing the notion that change begins at the personal level and can ripple outward to create meaningful societal shifts.

Hope for a More Rational Society

In the contemporary landscape, where misinformation spreads rapidly through social media and traditional media channels, the prospect of cultivating a more rational society may seem daunting. However, the emergence of critical thinking initiatives and digital literacy programs offers a beacon of hope. These initiatives aim to equip individuals with the tools necessary to discern credible information from falsehoods, fostering a population that values reason over emotion. By prioritizing education that emphasizes analytical skills, we can begin to counteract the pervasive influence of sensationalism and polarization.

Community engagement plays a crucial role in restoring rational discourse. Grassroots movements that promote open dialogue and respectful debate can help bridge the divides created by echo chambers. Encouraging diverse viewpoints and fostering environments where differing opinions can be aired without hostility can lead to a more nuanced understanding of complex issues. This communal effort can cultivate empathy and respect, essential components for a rational society where individuals are willing to listen and learn from one another.

The role of the education system cannot be overstated in this endeavor. Institutions must adapt their curricula to include critical thinking as a core component, teaching students not only how to evaluate sources but also how to engage in constructive discussions. Educators should be trained to facilitate conversations that promote inquiry and skepticism, rather than rote memorization of facts. By instilling these skills in the next generation, we can nurture a populace that prioritizes reasoned argumentation over emotional reactions.

Moreover, the responsibility also lies with media organizations to strive for higher standards of journalism. By adhering to ethical practices and prioritizing fact-checking, media outlets can rebuild the trust that has been eroded by sensationalist reporting. Transparency about sources and methodologies can empower audiences to make informed decisions about the information they consume. As consumers of news become more discerning, the demand for quality journalism may encourage media companies to prioritize substance over sensationalism.

Lastly, fostering hope in a more rational society requires collective action from all sectors of society. Individuals must take personal responsibility for their information consumption, actively seeking out credible sources and engaging with diverse perspectives. By joining forces with educators, media professionals, and community leaders, we can create a culture that values rational discourse and critical thinking. While the challenges are significant, the commitment to nurturing a more informed and rational society is not only possible but essential for the future of democracy and social cohesion.

www.ingramcontent.com/pod-product-compliance
Lightning Source LLC
Chambersburg PA
CBHW061533250726
48657CB00005B/2210